HIEROGRAPHYX

Afro-Futuristic Inspired Coloring Book

MICAH WILSON
AUTHOR & ILLUSTRATOR

HIEROGRAPHYX ART & DESIGN
PUBLISHER

www.hierographyx.com

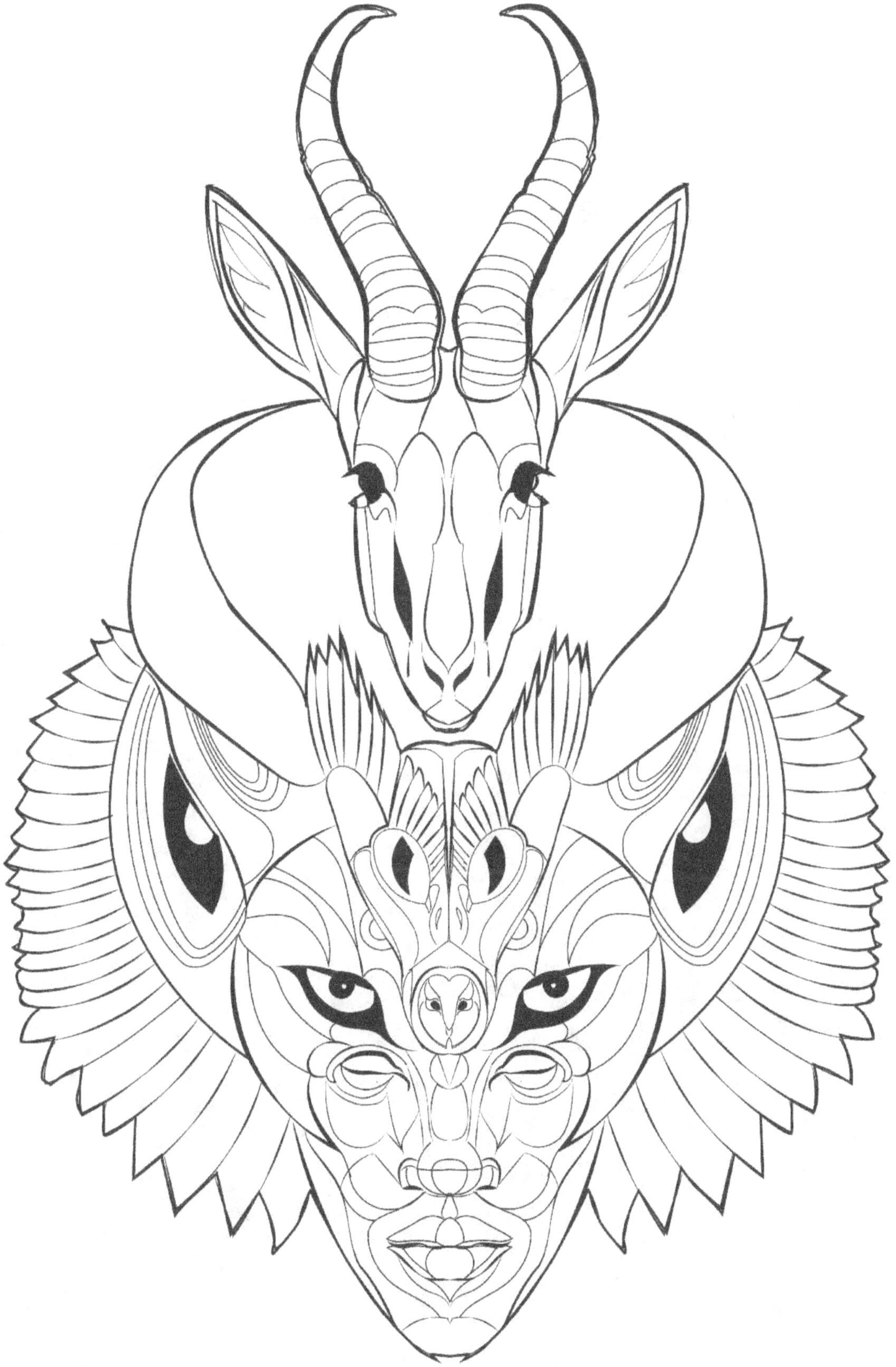

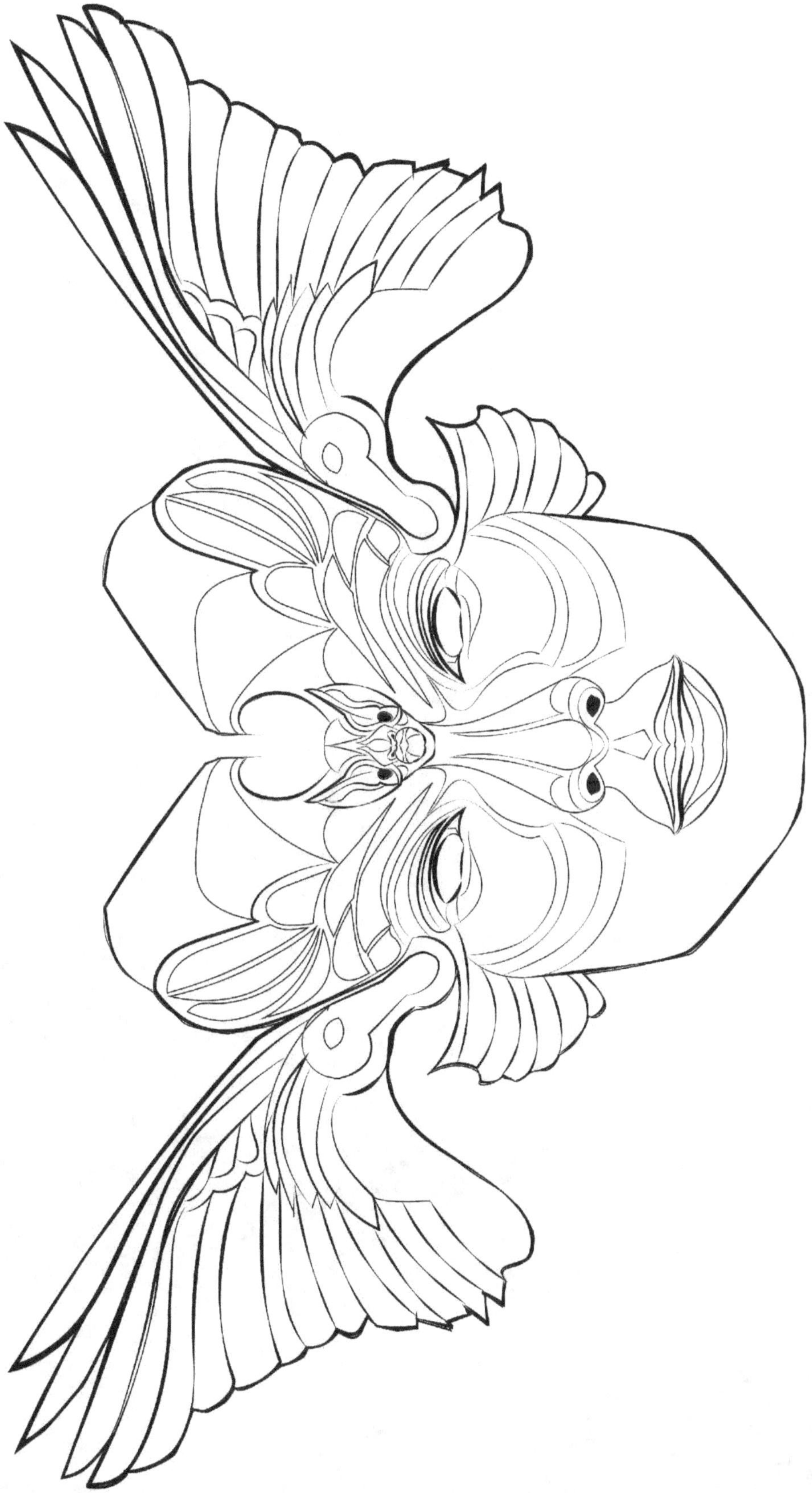

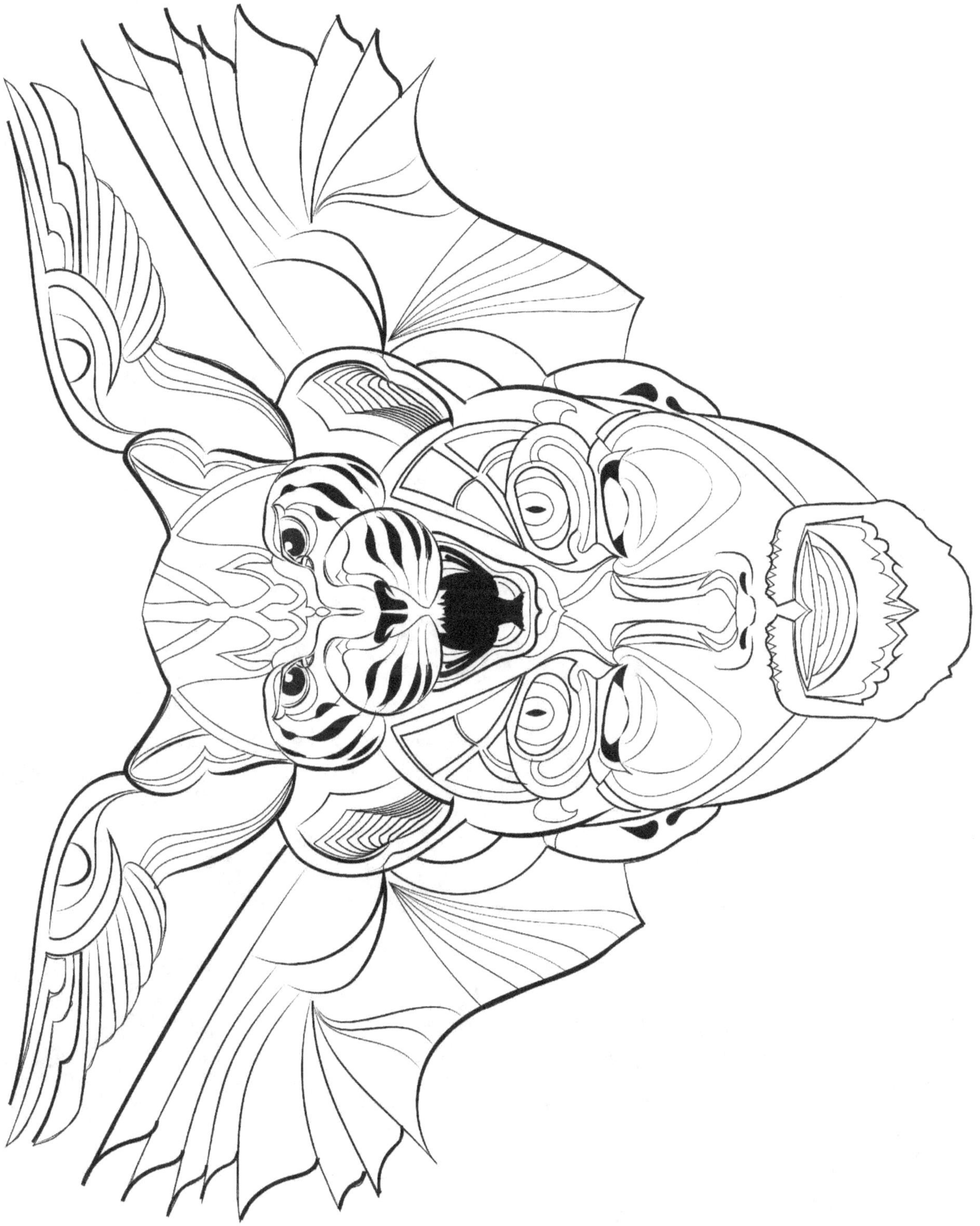

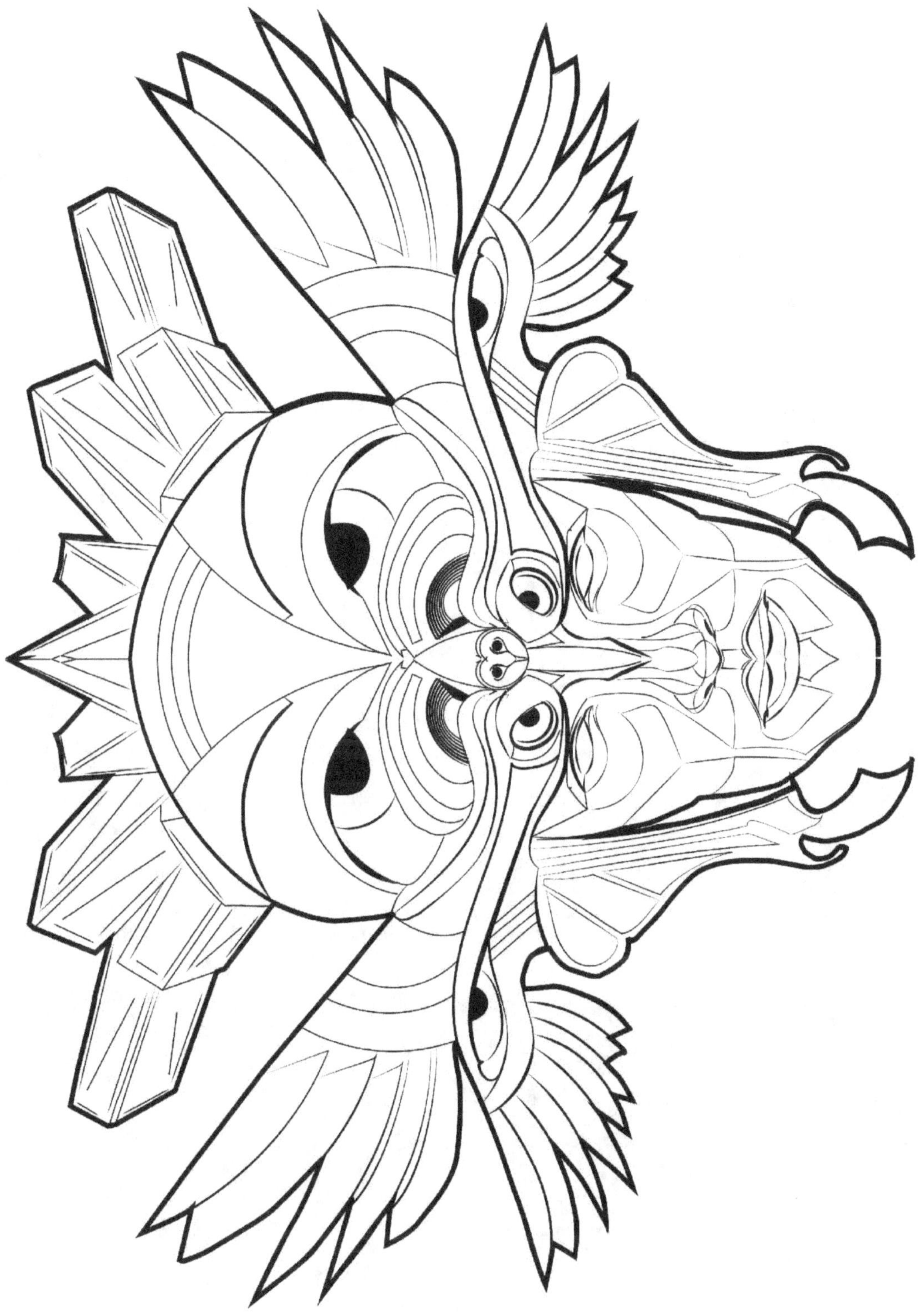

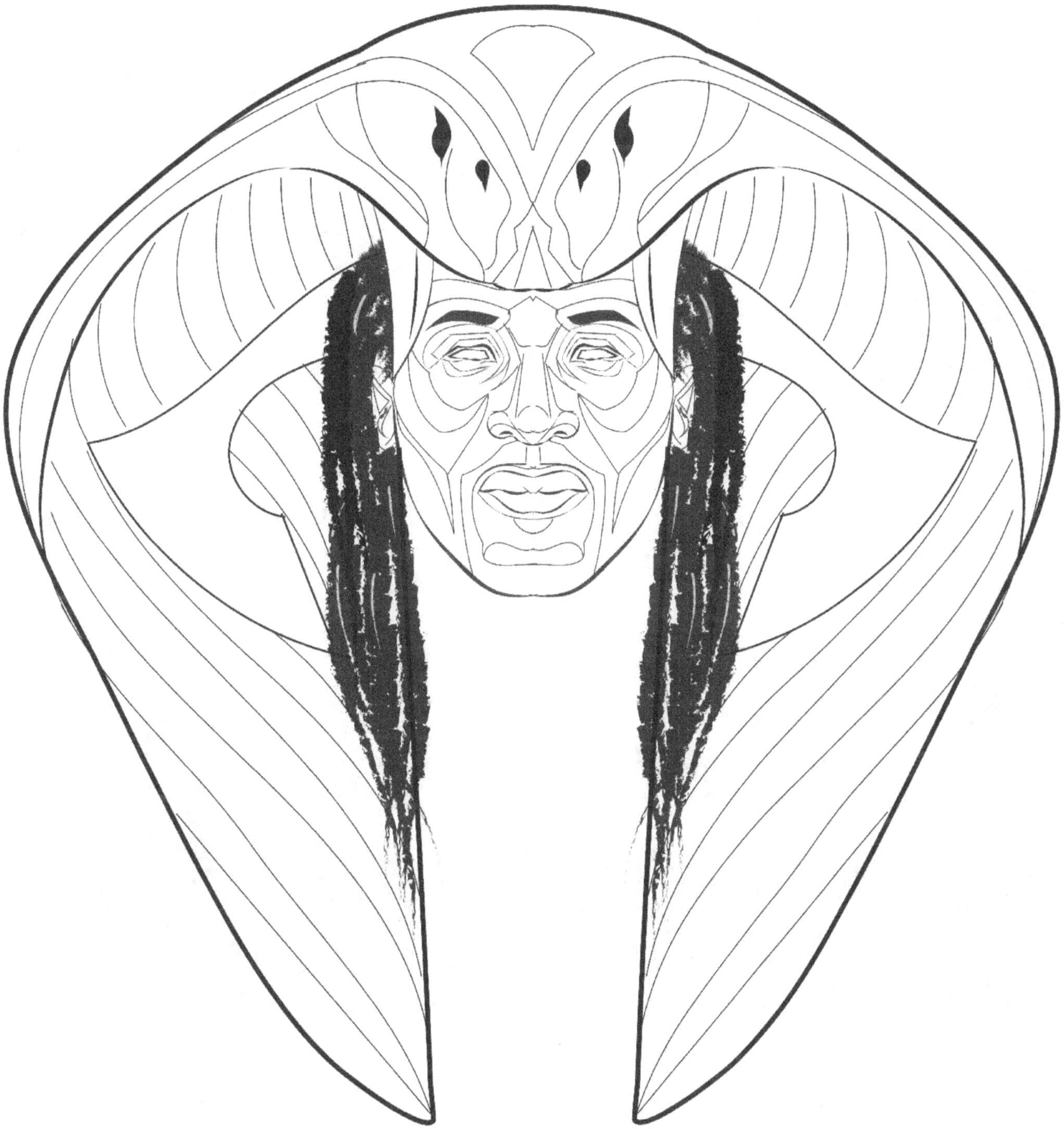

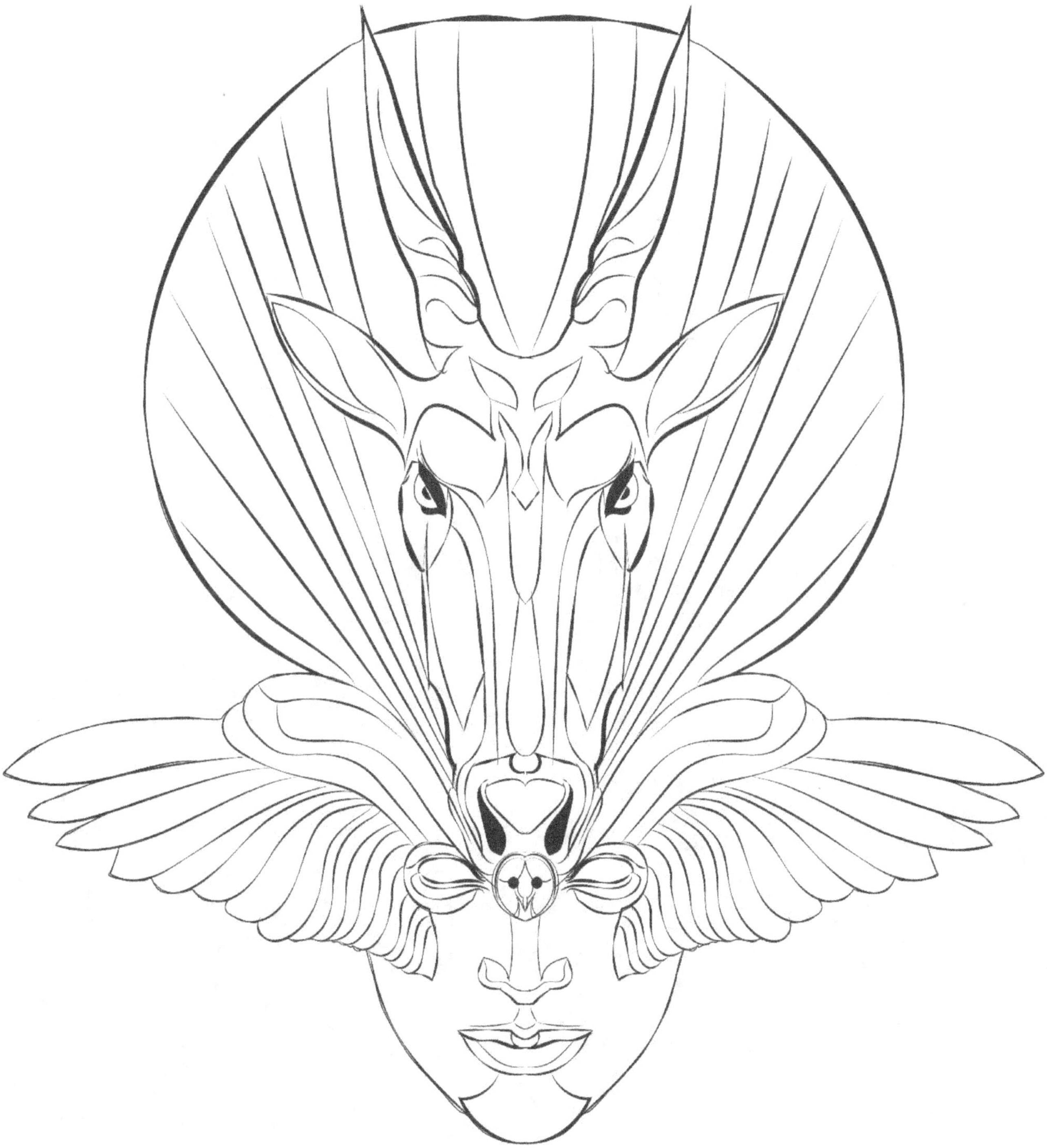

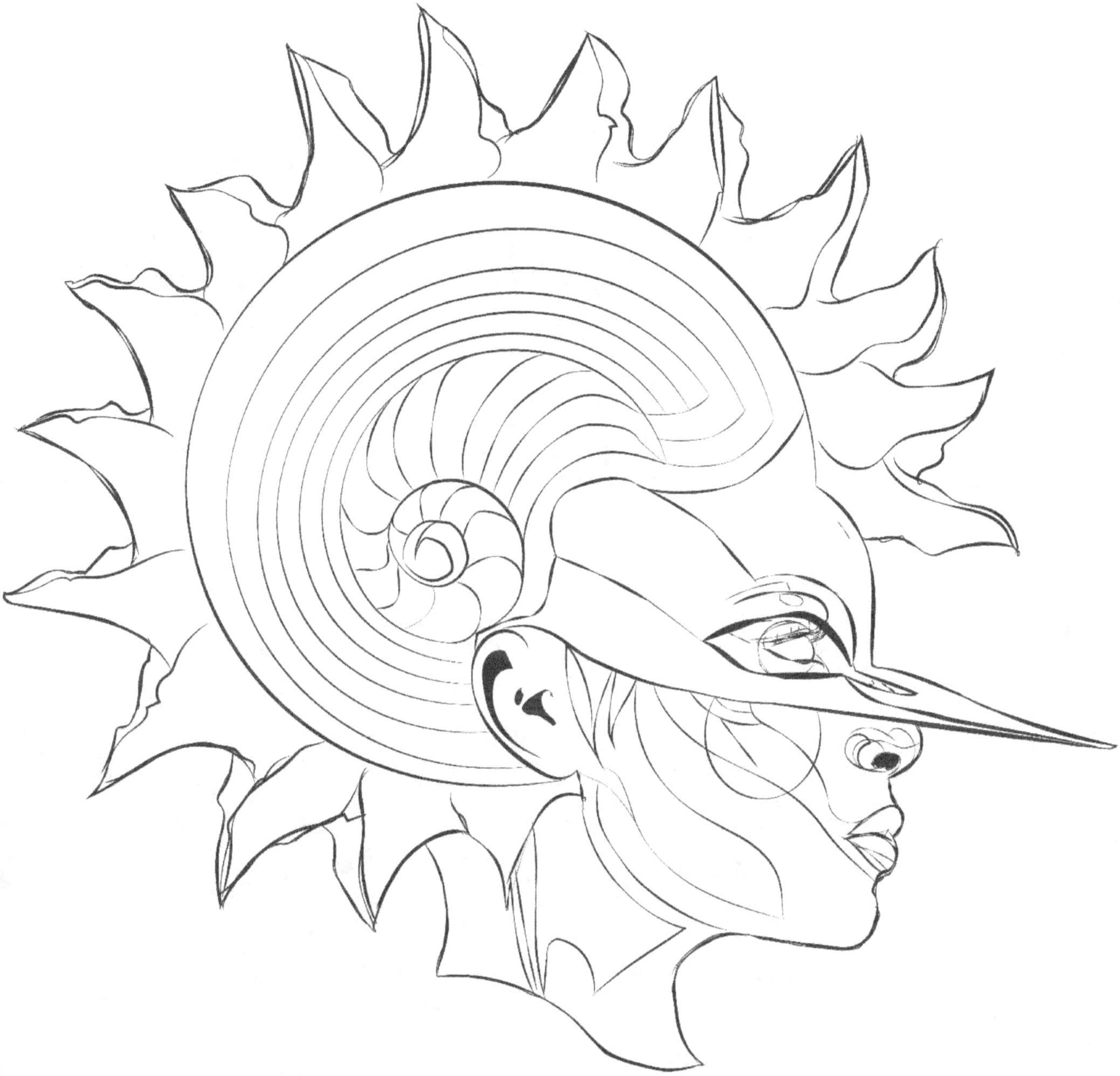

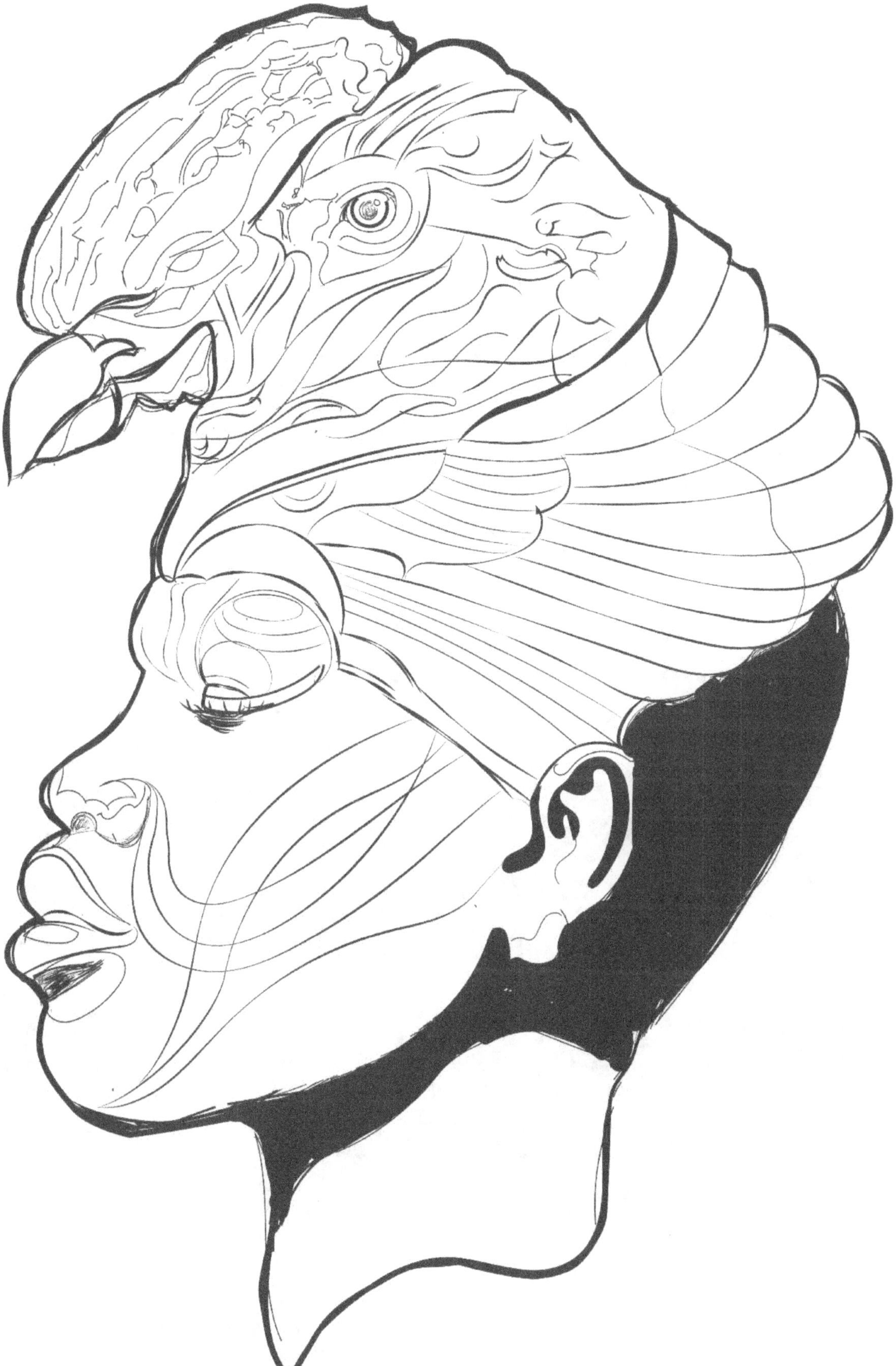

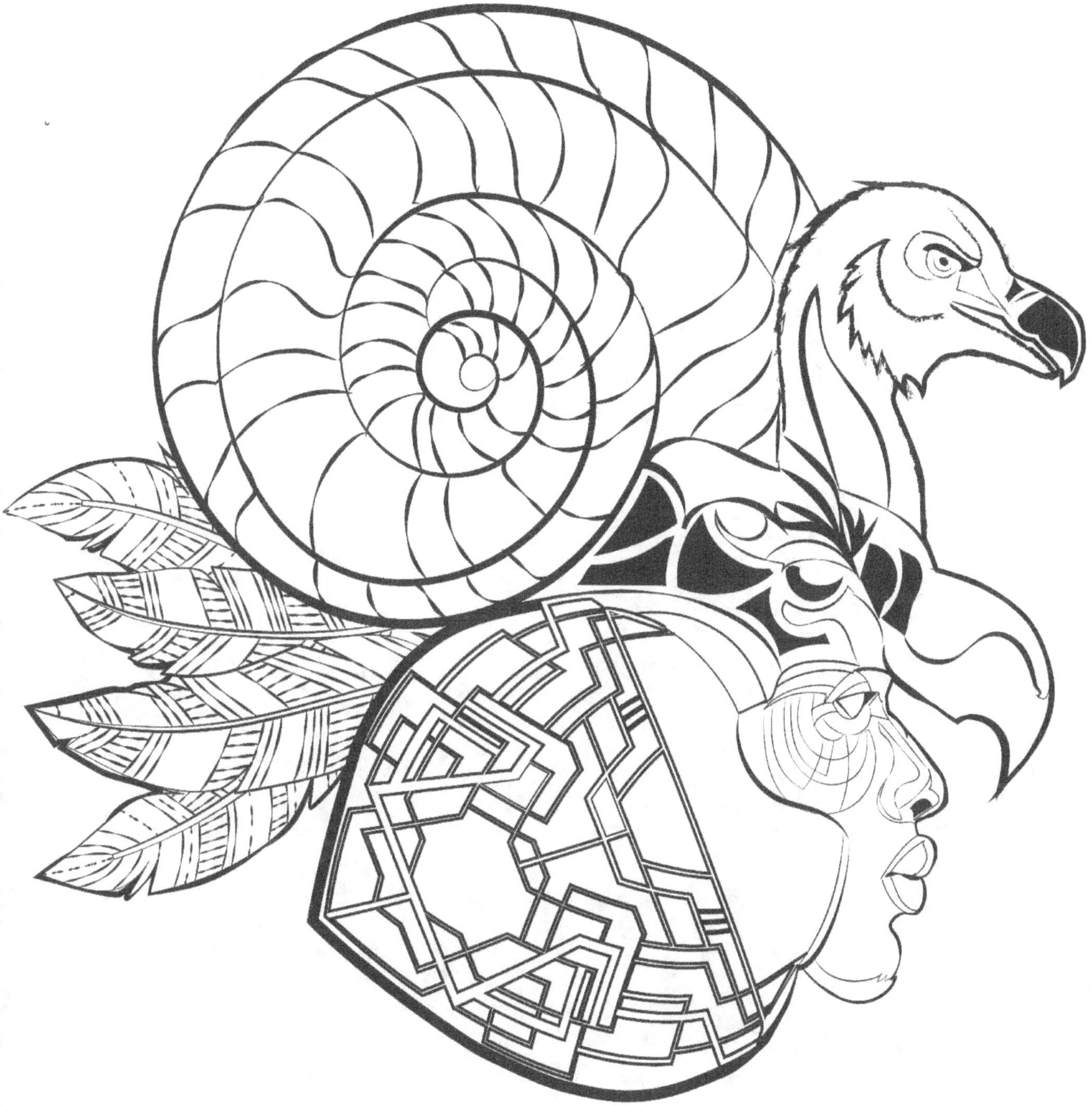

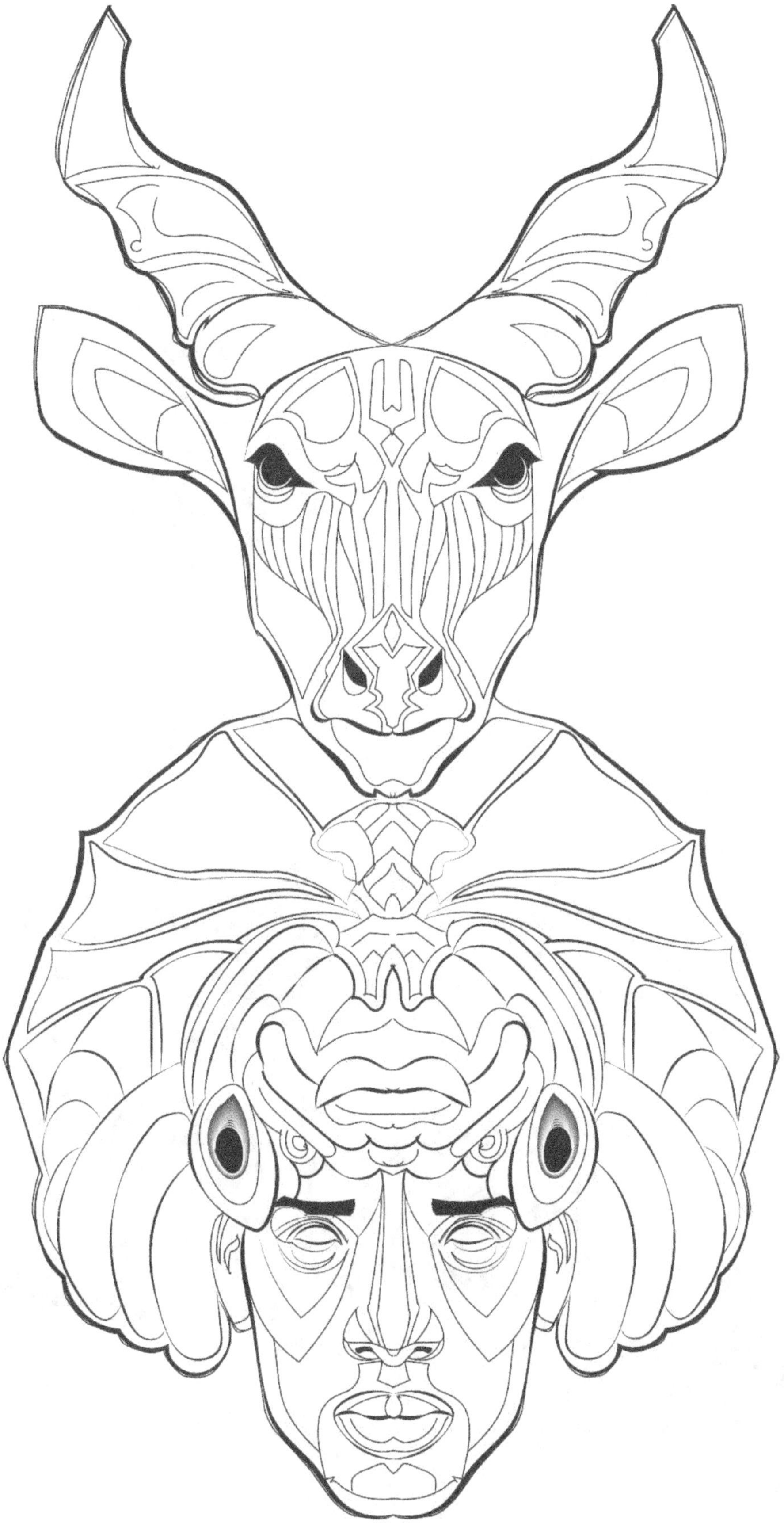

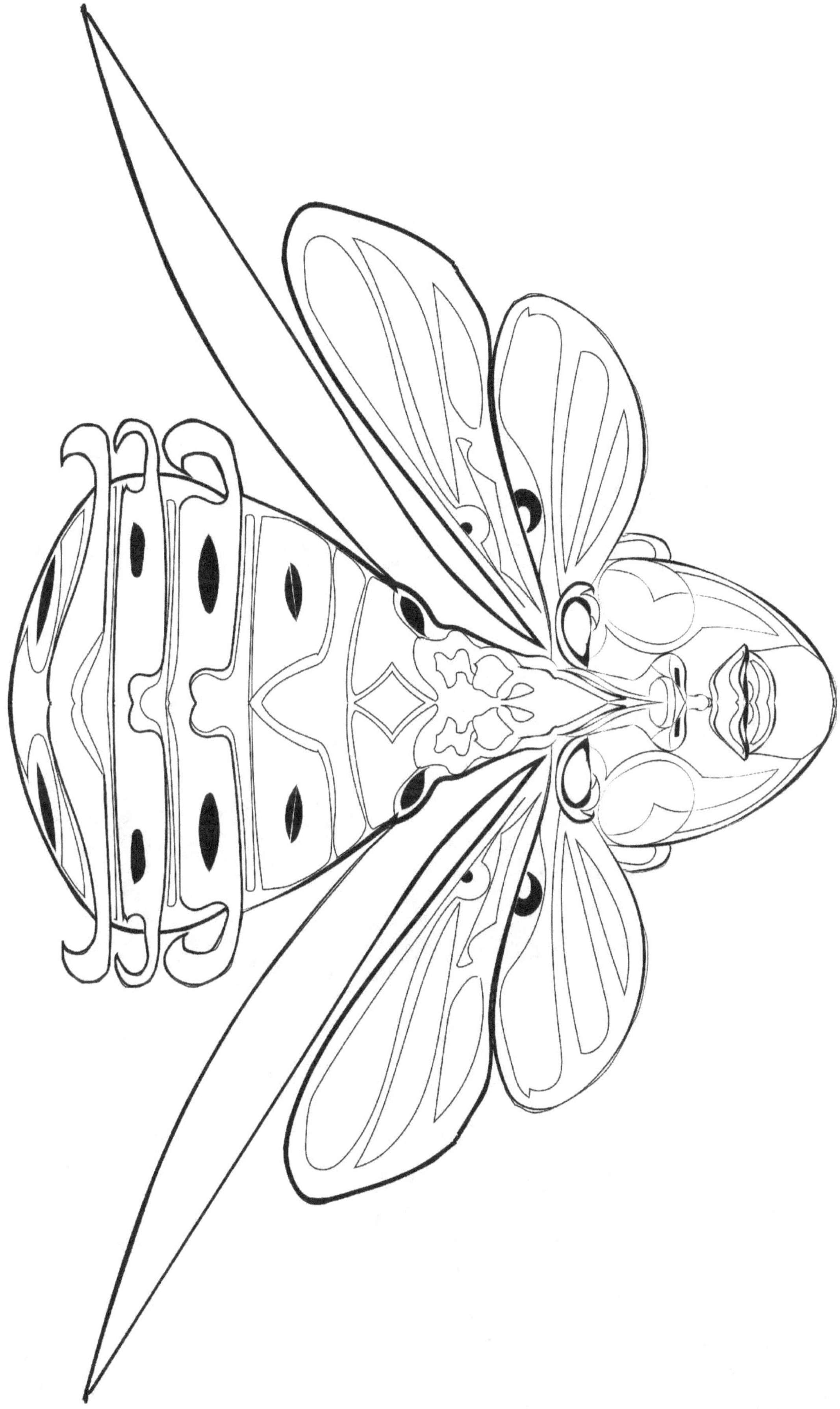

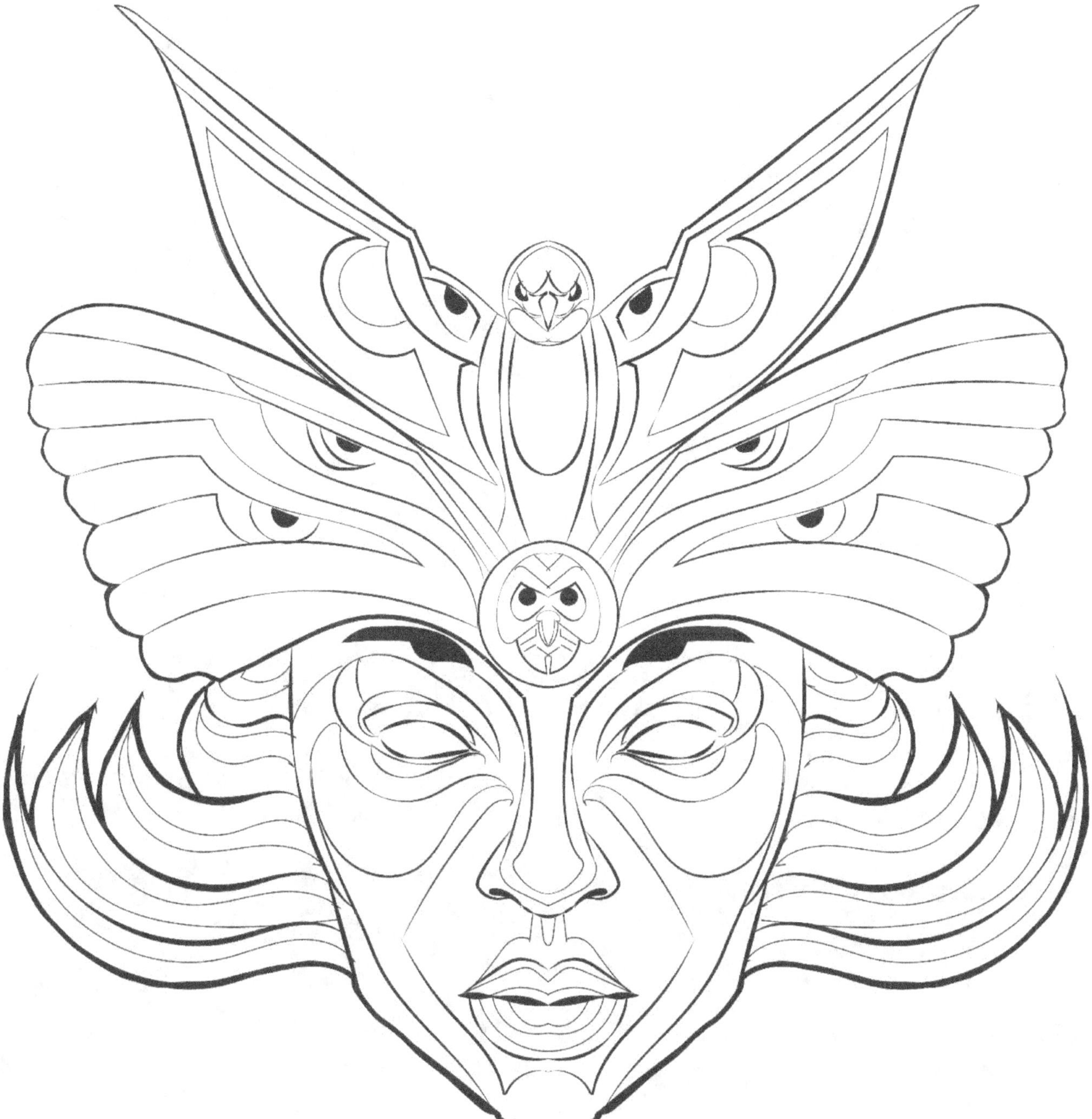

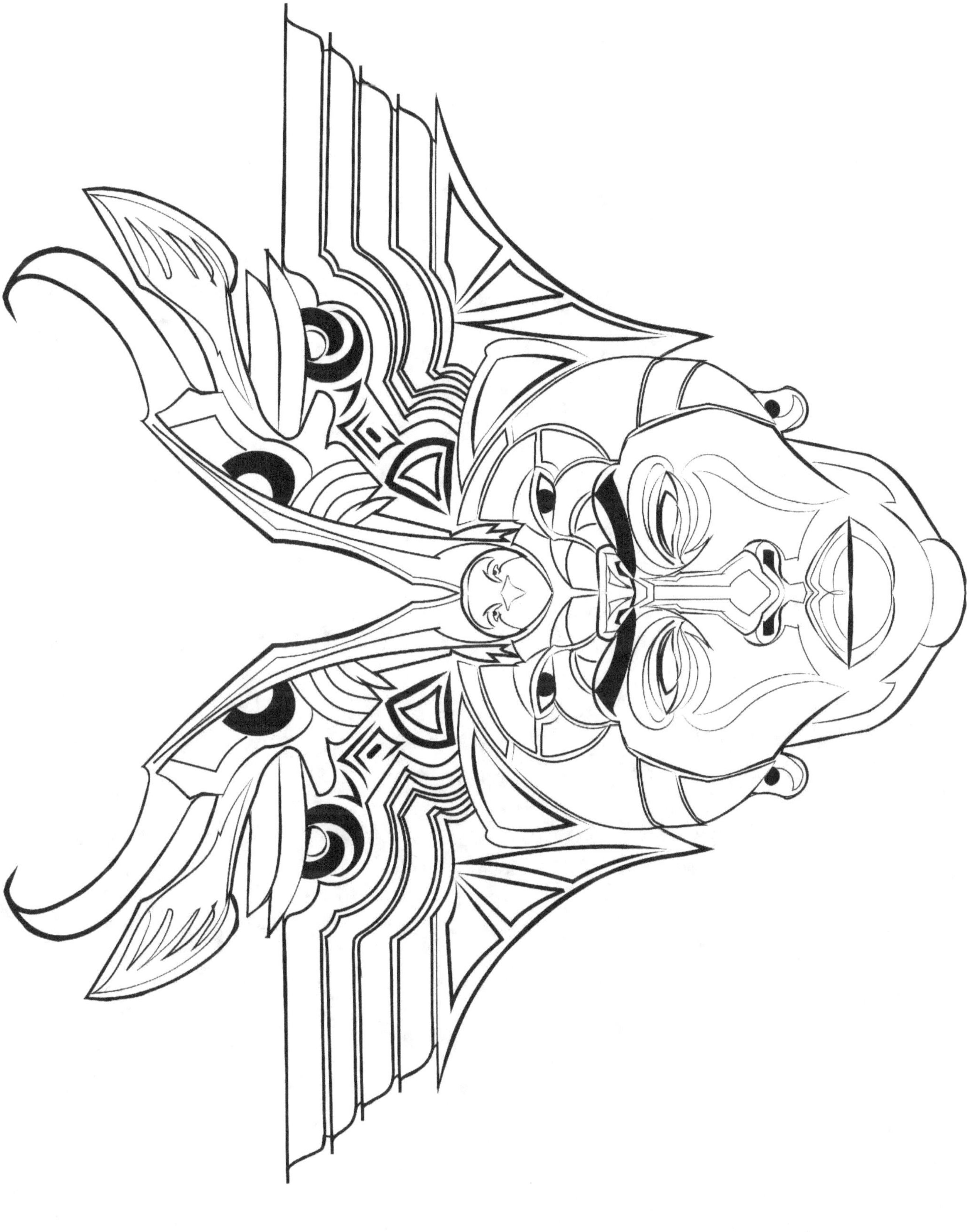

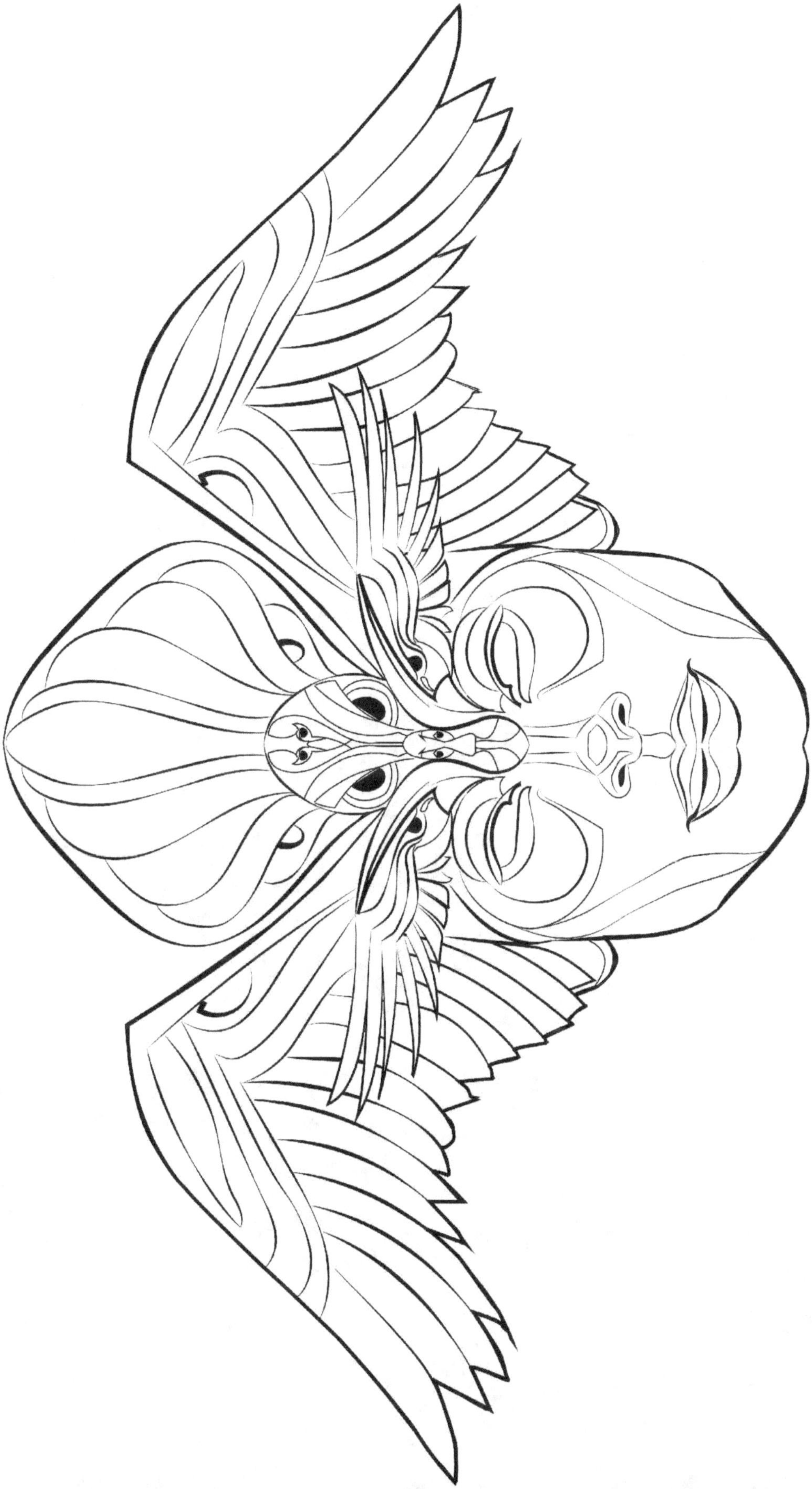

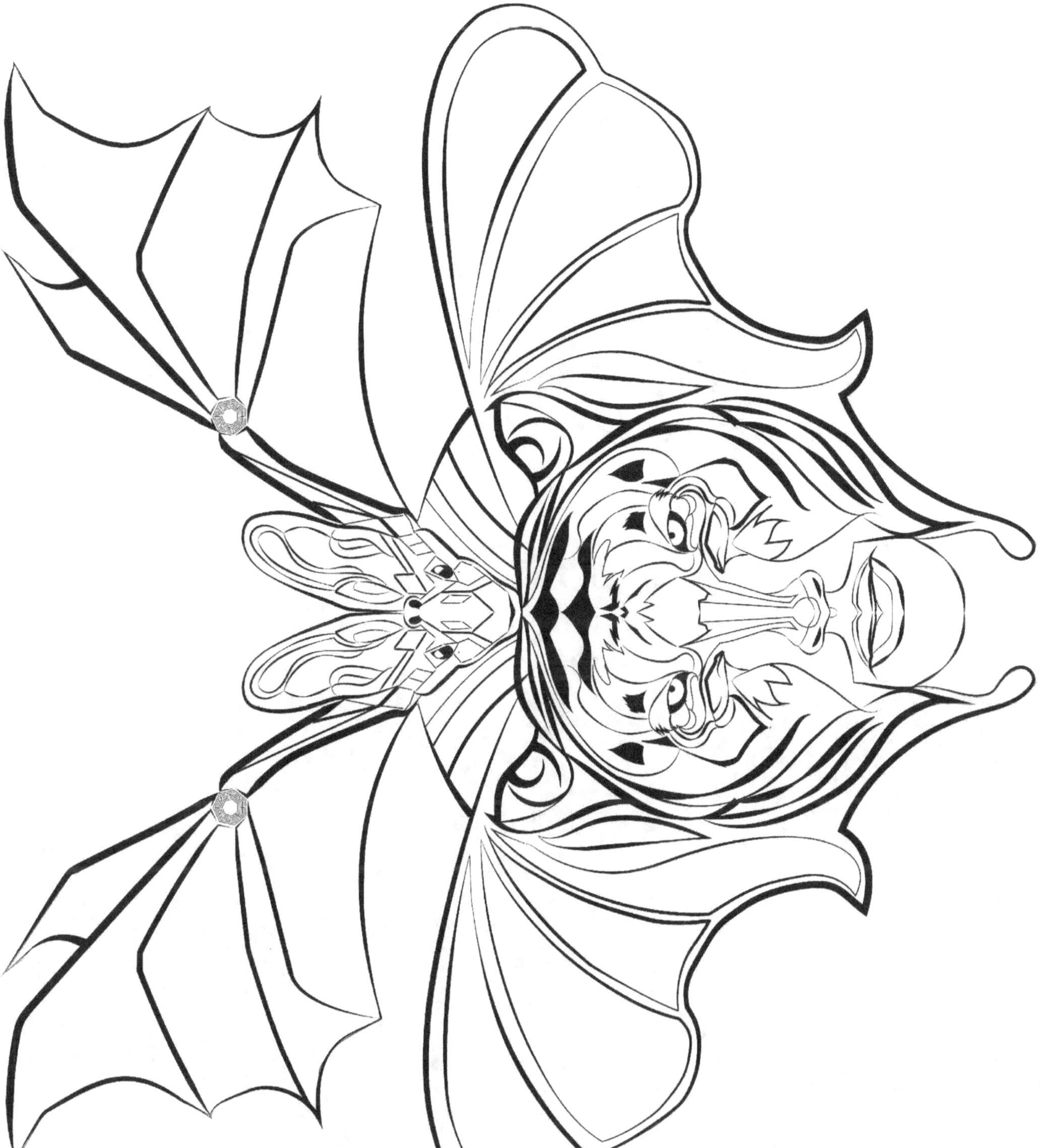

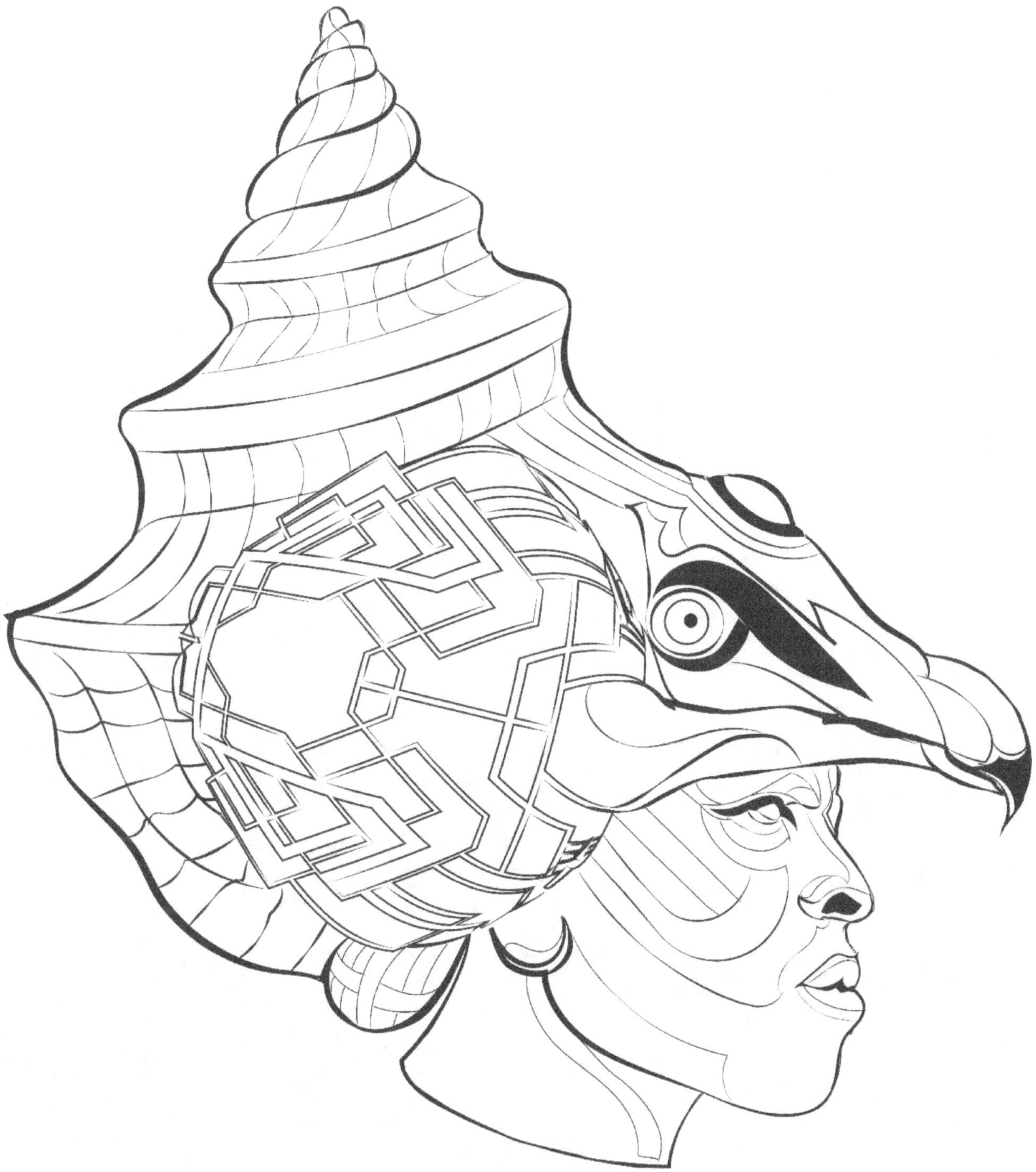

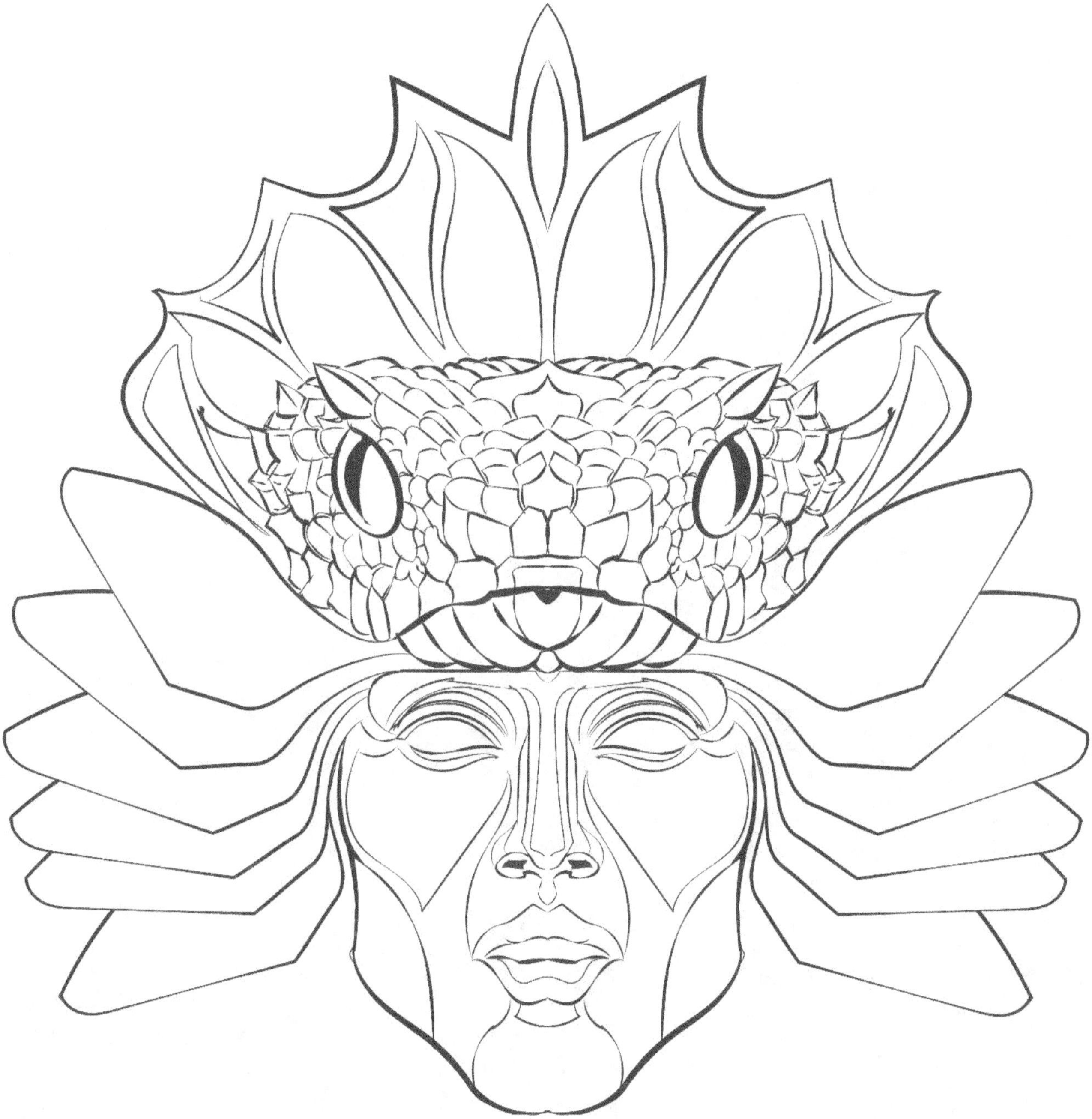

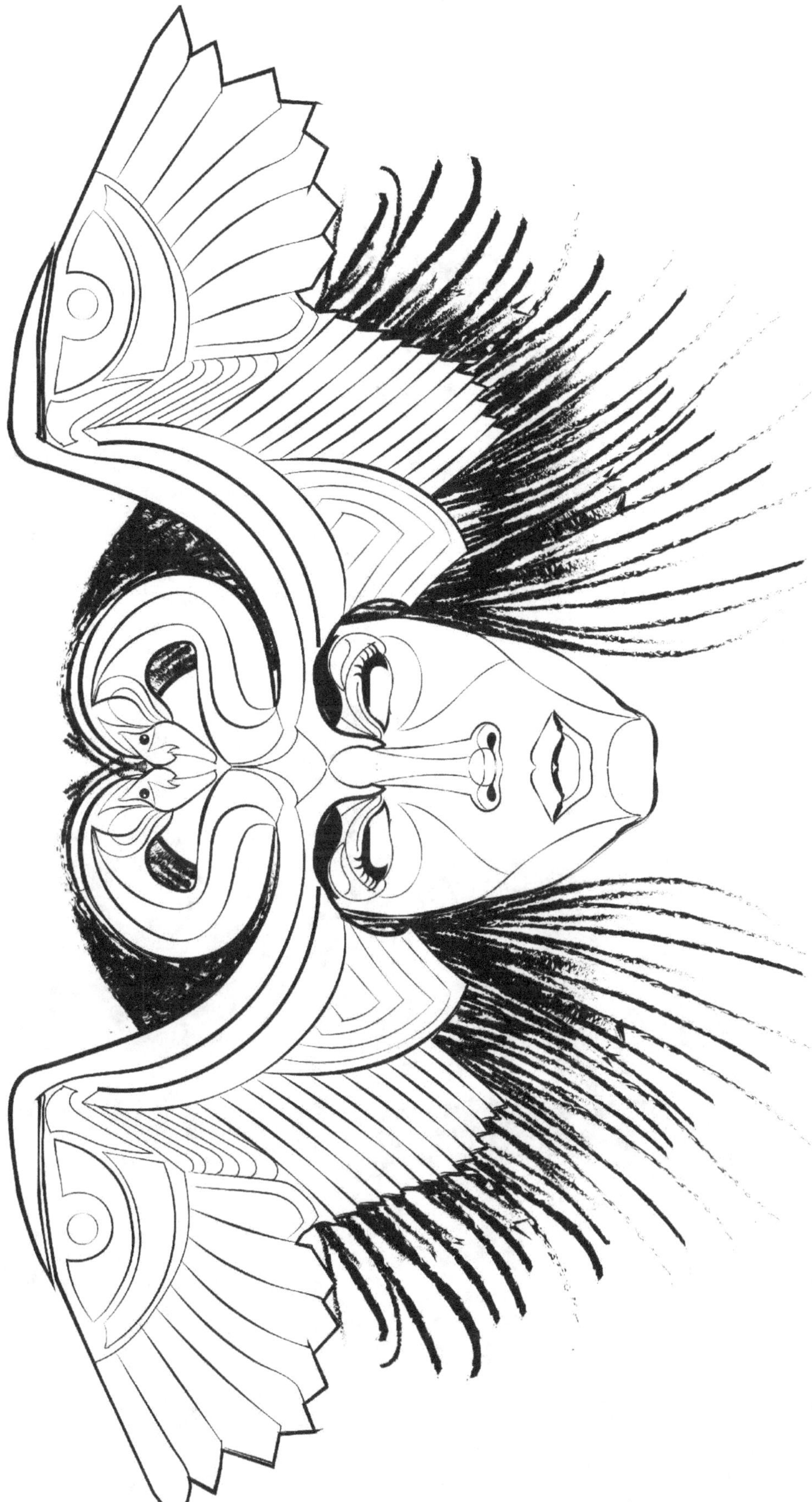

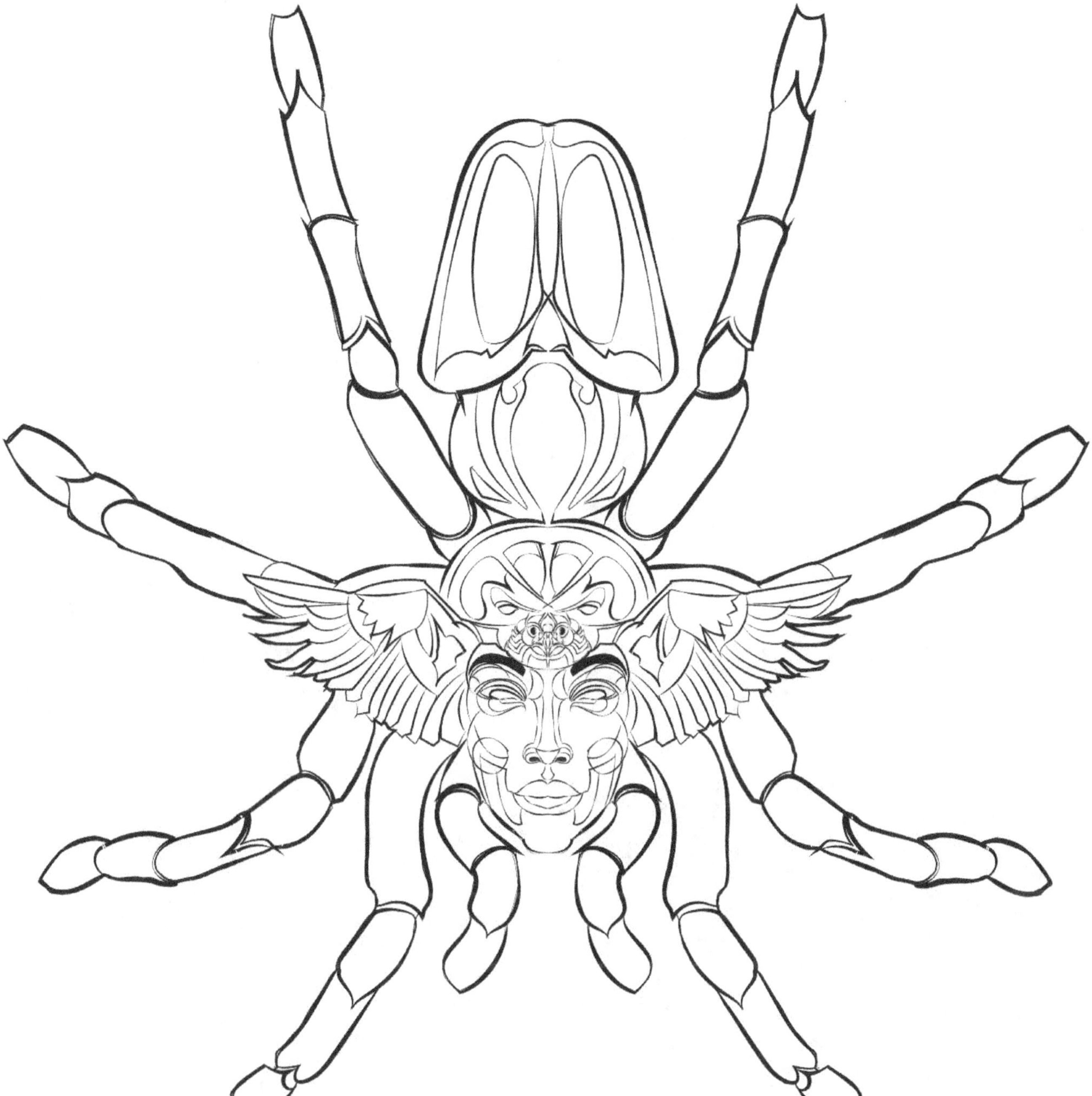

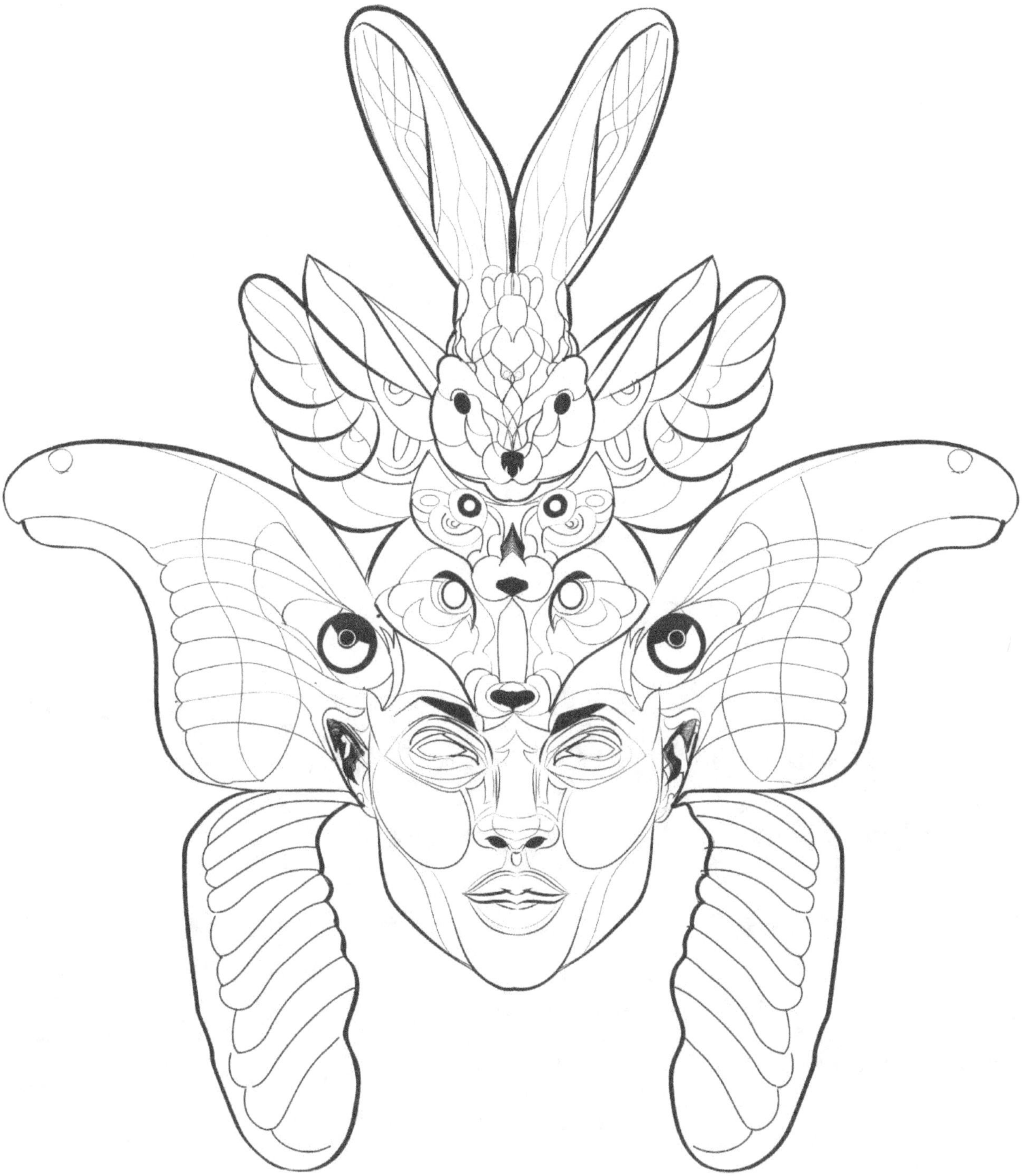

www.ingramcontent.com/pod-product-compliance
Lightning Source LLC
Chambersburg PA
CBHW081647220526
45468CB00009B/2573

* 9 7 8 1 7 2 2 8 4 9 9 1 7 *